Further Praise for
Daddy Daughter Dinner Dance

"Having experienced this book I can't decide if it is a book about a father's dedication and love for his beautiful daughter, or a book about two Artists, both very old souls, come together to share their insights, passions and profound experience of truth, with us all. India's art opens our minds as Bill's words open our hearts. On this wonderful new-family journey, we are touched to open a little piece of ourselves. Enjoy." —Shauna Hoffman, MA, MFT

"Bill Quateman shares nuggets of his life fathering India in this gentle book of personal reflections. Single parents may find comfort in the unique journey of this father daughter duo."

—Mimi Doe, author of *Busy but Balanced* (St. Martin's Press) and *10 Principles for Spiritual Parenting* (HarperCollins). spiritualparenting.com

"Bill's book reminds us of the profundity and importance of one of humankind's most vital relationships—that between a father and daughter. Their relationship is inspiring."

—Catherine DeMonte, MFCC

"Your book is terrific and is completely sensitive to the father daughter relationship. The concept of your daughter's artwork coupled with your poetic words is bound to capture the hearts of fathers and daughters (and moms too!) across the country."

—Richard H. Axel, DCSW, author of *A Father's Love, A Daughter's Power* available from Axel Publications

". . . the book and its message. . . . What a brilliant idea!"

—June Podagrosi, Executive Director of Child's Play Touring Theatre

"*Daddy Daughter Dinner Dance* is a portrait of love. It celebrates the richness and joy of conscious parenting. If only more childrens' awakenings to the world were held in this gentle embrace."

—Laura Ferris, India's Kindergarten Teacher, Highland Hall Waldorf School

"In Bill and India, we see the wonderful testimonial of the love between a father and daughter—and much more. Bill shares the essence of parenting and how a parent's love transcends family structure and the multitude of daily, adult concerns to focus on the sweetness of childhood. He reminds us to take the time to revel in this joy."

—Mark T. Rolewski, Area One Director, Success For All Foundation

Daddy Daughter Dinner Dance

Daddy Daughter Dinner Dance

A Father's Steps to a Blended Family That Really Works

Bill Quateman & India

Angel Mind

International Standard Book Number: 0-9729866-0-X
Library of Congress Control Number: 2003092070

Published by
Angel Mind, Inc.
P.O. Box 56301
Sherman Oaks, CA 91413
USA
818.424.2619
www.angelmind.net

Cover and interior design: **Bill Fate**
Edited by **Cynthia Dagnal-Myron**
Production manager: **Terry Stone**
Cover photography: **Robert Kazandjian**

Printed in Hong Kong

Photo of India on page 15 and of Lucille on page 26 by Henry Diltz

Contents

Acknowledgments

I'd like to thank the following people for the tremendous contributions they've made to my knowing about family, kids and taking care of each other and without whom this would have been a different book, written by someone else. All of us together, make this story.

- India, Dylan and Lucille, my kids, for being the realist life lessons of all. You are my treasures.
- Alice Quateman, my mother, for being the unconditional runaway Love Machine.
- Frank Skorodin, my grandfather, for being the supreme goofball pioneer and the Landlord of Love.
- The Señor, my teacher, for his over soul inspiration by showing the way.
- Catherine DeMonte, our family psycho-spiritual consigliere, for her largeness of heart and insight into family and children.
- Tim Craig, founder and director of Children's Circle Pre-School, for teaching us the basics.
- Gary Quateman, my brother, for his kindness, support, room and board.
- Andy Frances, my friend and manager, for his help and integrity.
- Cynthia Dagnal-Myron, for her tremendous writing and shamanic talents and her heart & soulship.
- Patricia Quateman and Tammy Grady, mothers of the kids, for being open hearted, great parents and good friends, really.
- Selma Brown, my aunt, for showing me art and living it and having the courage to take me around when I was 6 years old.
- Wendy Iscove and Vera Mazzeo, my playgroup, for showing me what great parenting was like.
- Neil Quateman, my brother, for his steadfastness and accountableness.

MVP

Bernadette Heyer

Purple Hearts of Caring

Lauren & Kermit Aguayo, Leslie & Bill McNutt, Terry Stone, Bob Zeman, Megon McDonough, Maggie Gautier

Stand By Me Awards

Jay Levinson, Phil Mitchell, Jill Harker, Rio Phior, Eva Quateman, Marc & Noa Shinderman, Lisa Quateman

Introduction

Daddies, Daughters and "The Dance"

A daddy is his daughter's first dance partner, pretty literally. Love, Joseph Campbell tells us, enters first through the eyes. A loving look between partners is where all classic ballets begin. Remember Tony and Maria in the dance at the gym from *West Side Story*?

A girl gets what it's like to be valued by a man through the look in her father's eyes, mostly during the first 5 years. Psychologically, that's where she sets up her knowledge, which turns into expectations, of how a man will treat her. This "eye love you dance" that she does with her Daddy is what she will look for in the partners that show up later in her life. And while she might think: "I want a guy just like my Daddy," I think it's truly: "I want a guy that moves me like my Dad."

We say: "when the spirit moves you." This spirit of moving is the underlying agreement to dance that a Father and a daughter engage in, mostly, I think, unknowingly. Certainly his touch, his caring and psychological environment, his way of being affects how she will expect men to be with her.

Men are generally more physical in their way of being with their children anyway. There's the classic scene at the playground where the babies want to be adventurous on some of the equipment and the Mothers will typically be very protective while the Fathers encourage the children to "Go to the next step, c'mon, you can do it!" I've delighted in holding and rocking my babies to sleep—my son and my daughter. But it was me and India "taking chances," climbing the spiral and swinging on the rings, that was the beginning of The Dance. That physical way of being together—tickling, wrestling, tosses on the couch or bed, swinging by the arms, riding horsey, back and shoulder rides—is the essence of dance.

I mean look at the Jitter Bug or Boogie Woogie—a fun one to teach a little girl to say, let alone do ("OK Indi, can you say, Boogie Woogie?"). These dances feature guys hurling their girls through the air with the greatest of ease and everybody loves it. Whenever I get physical with Indi she always says, "Do eet again." Now if repetition is not the nature of the dance, I don't know what is!

Having started a family at a later stage in life than most—I was 40 when Dylan was born and 48 when India was born—perhaps I see what we do together, the life we make with each other, more as a musical give and take, than a rush through work and parenting that comes with younger families. I feel more available to appreciation and fascination, perhaps.

And as a helplessly committed songwriter and musician (who do you have to have sex with to get out of this business?), everything is music to me: melody, nuance, heart-aching harmonies, phrasing, themes and rhythms. And being with my little partner on the dance floor of our lives is an enchantment.

As a single parent, concentrating on career, creativity and kids—our kids are our most creative endeavor—it is easy to focus on my own satisfaction with my daughter as the woman in my life. I have friendly, healthy relationships with the mothers of my children (there are two). I'm not dating or involved with an adult female. And I can see where the classic set up: an unhappy marriage yielding an unnatural and unhealthy relationship in which the father gets his emotional satisfaction from his daughter, could be an issue.

Yet ours is clear and uncluttered, due, perhaps, to the perspective and understanding I have of my own development as well as my daughter's.

Awareness, as usual, is the key. There is music in knowing.

The Source: A Dedication

Love comes from somewhere, and my love came from Alice.

Her father, Frank, was the great goofy "seer." His first daughter, my mother, Alice Skorodin, was born on a farm in Poland as he and his wife, Mary, were escaping the Jewish persecutions in Russia in 1922.

By the time I was born, my grandfather had three daughters. So I was the son he'd always wanted and I grew up in a house with my mother, father, both grandparents and two aunts. And for three years my feet did not touch the ground. My love starts in that house, with Frank (Froyim in Yiddish) as the producer and director of the love force that permeated both the house and my child's heart. When he died—I was 18—I cried like the baby that remembered his love.

My grandfather's loving-kindness was deeply planted in Alice, where it grew and flourished. We called her the Queen of Love. Yes, my two brothers and I are good boys who love their mother. Yet there is far more to Alice's caring for people; it transcended the family boundary. Alice made everyone she met feel comfortable and respected. The children flocked to her, the younger adults wished she was their mother (she'd always accept when asked if she would be), her friends adored her and the elderly gladly received her care and attention. Alice was, and remains, a woman for all ages.

Let's be real, though: Alice was a housewife for the better part of 30 years, raising three boys (oh my god) and dispensing good cheer and "lovingness" just about all that time. Shopping and cleaning and cooking and schlepping. Looking back now, it's clear she was clueless, as she would say, but heart-enlightened. Alice came from the heart her whole life. She was a woman and that's what women do. For sure.

But the best do it fully. And Alice was the Unconditional Queen. When my father wanted to leave her and move to Las Vegas with his secretary of many years—he'd had a "life changing" heart attack—Alice could have crumbled after devoting all of her prime, young adult life to her family. Her boys were almost all off to college; her husband had left her for another woman. But Alice had an "offensive heart attack" of her own, and went on to date and have two more relationships, the last of which, when she was 70 years old, was the love of her life. Alice was the "Queen of Can Do."

She, like my grandfather, was there for the laughs and the hugs and the kisses. For her, the greatest pleasure in the world was being in the company of the people she loved the most. Our toast at holiday meals was to "know that the miracle is being in the same room with the people that you love." Seeing her grandchildren, any children, unfolding through life's little plays and dramas, was a nutrient for her. These simple yet profound life interactions with people were her sustenance, her preference. They brought life to life for her.

And this is her great lesson, her legacy. True love is "being here." And when we are being here, in that love, we *are* the compassion we all long to feel and we *know* the security of sureness about being loved; it is what we must have in order to give it. And we can give it to anyone. "From your mouth to God's ears," was the core of the practical religion I got from her. In her living, Alice gave us all the lesson of being and giving love.

I take care of Alice a little bit, when I take care of my daughter. "Mythologically" this is true—and "actually" it is, too. This is the gift of love Alice keeps on giving her granddaughter as it comes through her father. It is the ancient Quantum connection. Even though she's not here, her love is running wild and filling people.

Little boats on the pond, in the wind
while admirers of the regatta
watch, motionless, with great hopes
and without breathing
from the shore

—Bill Quateman

A Showgirl

that gold ring
is
something to be–
the fashion look–
and one in her lip.

a no-sleeve dress
at 12 o'clock,
on her way to a meeting
wearing a ring and pearl bracelet
with a bow
in her hair

she has no idea in her eyes.

India's Pictures

I merely took the energy it takes to pout and wrote some blues.
—Duke Ellington, musician and composer (1899–1974)

I am no authority on art. I am an authority on what charms me. And India's faces, the ones that she drew, flashed and claimed a section of my heart.

I find in some of her drawings, not only a peek into who she is as a young lady emotionally and spiritually, but also a glimpse of Life. She captures a little magic and light—and it started with her faces.

My aunt, who is a muralist, folk, fine and graphic artist her whole life, agreed, on seeing a few drawings, that we had a bright eye on hand. She's telling stories, often, with her drawings. Even if it's a single figure, she'll say where it came from before this page. I often hear her talking or singing while she draws. I hear in beats and melodies anyway, so both of us are lucky to have each other.

All engaging and intriguing images or sounds have instant joy or pathos and boundlessness about them, an abandon that lands easily on its elegance in communicating the message of humanness and universal connectedness of our experiences here. This is how we teach each other to be humans.

Children, just as they come to us, have this creative abandon that we, in our best moments of parenting, can coax and invite into free expression by creating an atmosphere where they feel safe in being who they are, and at ease in discovery. Of course, all while being guided—like a dance, a lean here, a stop there, bend and swoop and bow.

Doin' the great Universal.

So, India's drawings remind me of this, aliveness. We both like thinking about it. We're making with our time, a soul container to keep stuff live inside.

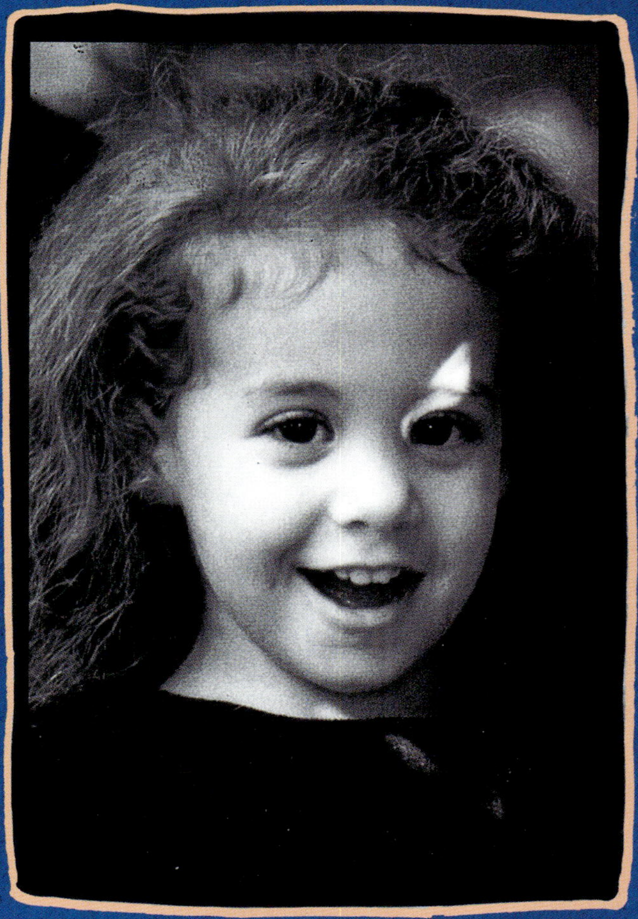

Not a Good Day

There was a
thunderstorm
and the house
broke
her brother was
out of the house
and there was

no umbrella.

Being There

The happiness of life is made up of minute fractions—the little, soon-forgotten charities of a kiss or smile, a kind look or heartfelt compliment
—Samuel Taylor Coleridge, poet and philosopher (1772–1834)

Our children, as ourselves, are born with innate likes and dislikes, predispositions or tendencies or predilections. As parents, to help our children flourish, we must: 1. Keep them safe, and 2. Care about what happens to them.

That is the stock for the recipe of self-esteem. Specifically how we do this is by developing our own awareness, being adventurous. We must also create stability and love in our own lives and offer this to our kids and anyone else within range, along with activities that develop these qualities—mind/body games of any sort. If they "bite," everybody's lucky.

If they don't bite, we bring other activities by. When they show enthusiasm for something, we pay attention to it, see if it flourishes. We are the servers, they are the lucky diners.

All this means that we must commit. We must give a certain amount of time to be with our kids to learn their language so we can be involved in the most important part of their lives, which is helping them to develop core beliefs and interests. There is really no such thing as spending quality time with people; there must be "present" time with people. If we are truly "with" our kids when we are with them (T-shirt: "*Be* with your kids when you're with them"), they will be nourished in the most basic of ways: they will feel that they matter to us. And they will know this completely and most powerfully without words.

We will have laid our bodies on the line and communicated the most important message: you are important and unique to me. And they will know this by the simple act of our attention. So it then becomes less important what games we play with our children—whether they are mind games or body games or both—than that we play games and tell stories and just goof with them, at all. We must find what charms our kids and help nurture their interest it. Teach them how exciting learning and growing are.

This is the giving we do. And if, as men, we follow our daughters' lead, they will waltz us into their hearts and minds. And in that connection lies the magic and power of relationship, and, some of the deepest joys on earth.

My Crown and Sunglasses

i'll sit
on my chair

and have my drink
with flowers
and a straw
in the sun

with my crown and sunglasses

by
the waterfall

waiting for you
to

join me

India

Somewhere, something incredible is waiting to be known.
—Carl Sagan, astronomer (1934–1996)

I wanted  **her name to sing.**

And to honor the spiritual connotations that India—the country and many of its "human messengers"—have brought to us, from the sublime poetry of Rabindrinath Tagore to the prophetic vision of Mahatma Gandhi to the majestic remoteness of Tibet to the real life magic of the Vedas and the Upanishads and the Buddha. Each telling us all, *we* are the miracle—most recently, by having Deepak Chopra and the Dalai Lama on our local PBS station to pass along the news.

India reminds me of this. A mixed manifestation.

She's a beauty from the inside out, a sweet and curious, attentive, goofy, playful, smart, generous, testy, controlling, loving, sensitive, creative child. Her Mom's side of the family is part Black, part Choctaw Indian, part German. Mine is Russian Jewish. She's a mix.

She's a little princess of the universe in training. She has a goofy laugh, especially when grabbed by the chicken arm. Or the chicken belly, or the chicken cheeks. Or the chicken neck (aka, neck chicken) or chicken tush. She likes to be thrown. Into the pool, onto the bed, makes no difference, god has his arm around her. This is how she lives her life, hurtling herself into the play area to start the playing immediately. Her curiosity is large and a thing of beauty.

She loves a good story, has infinite energy and mostly plays fair. She's a good mix. An angel on wheels; "the best girl in 7 states," as her Grandma used to say.

As for some of her talents—aside from raging cuteness—I am all prejudice, although I am a trained observer. She has an outstanding singing talent and I have two tapes of her singing "Twinkle Twinkle Little Star" about a year apart, at age 3 and 4, that kill. In fact, with her beauty and looks and talent, living in Los Angeles, she may find herself attracted to show business. I am prepared. I'll conduct my interviews of her suitors by the gun collection. I'm not afraid. I'll embarrass her a little. Her Dad's a dangerous guy.

She creates astonishing drawings and sketches. Her faces and figures have a character and clarity that give them a real style that is like her little soul, insightful, goofy, emotional and to the point.

India is a great play pal, finding fascination readily, drinking water at least some of the time without complaining—liking it really. She also knows how to whine and pout with great accuracy. She likes butterflies because of the chrysalis. The change attracts her. She pretends that she's one of our pussycats that died, Pudders, and we talk to him and tell him that we miss him and it's good to see him and we bet he's doing fine there in heaven and we like it and it feels good.

It is said that Indigo children are the ones that come with some sort of knowing sense of their being here. Perhaps slightly aware that they are aware. This would describe a part of her. She's a regular kid with frustrations, pouting, and tantrums on occasions, yet able to move through them, when guided, with ease. Peace in the midst of chaos.

That's where we need to be: Five-year-olds, close to Buddha nature. Given half the chance, they will do that naturally.

We can allow something incredible to be known.

Date Night

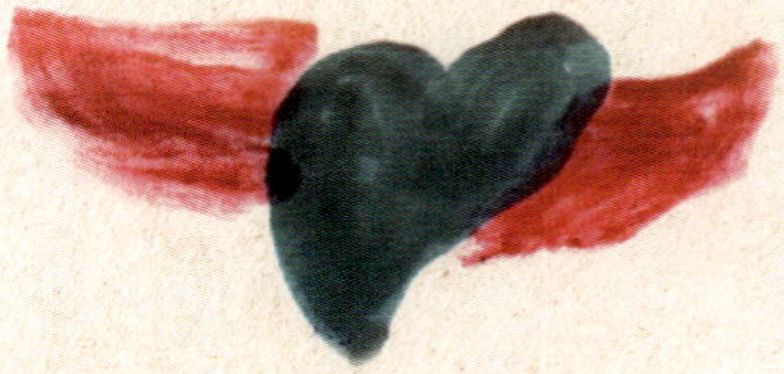

The twirl of lights and sounds, next-to-last Saturday summer night, eager parents and early lovers, teens in titillating outfits and glances (all style and cool), living in instant romance, expecting impossible fun, wide-eyed babes, angry overworked, undersupported black woman screaming for her 2 tickets to be returned because her boy didn't ride and he gave the young Hispanic boy running the roller coaster 3 tickets, not one, like he says, cotton candy carmel apple fantasies of fun, some falling short, the balls don't stay in the basket, so you don't get the stuffed toy for $5, feeling bad, so there's fun over here, screaming wildly on the spinning body throwing thing (this must be what it's like to be a hummingbird) with looks of love and delight through smiling devoted eyes in the twisting streaming night light backdrop.

Standing in the lines, holding both of my hands, nestled against the front of my legs, soaking in the life, just noticing, thinking on our own with intermittent exclamations, we made a hands in the air on the roller coaster life time memory out of watching the carnival together, on date night.

Daddy the Captain

Daddy the captain
  and India
the next captain

on a trip
  to get coconuts
because
  they're a furry, funny food.

Stepping In

In this house all must be friends, all must be loved,
all must be held dear, all must be helped.
—*St. Teresa of Avila (1515–1582)*

Lucille taught me the basics of parenting. She has been my introduction to fathering in a complex way. And like most good teachers, she was a tough one. Looking back, she is one of the main reasons I think of myself as a good Dad.

Her blood father is mulatto and English, her mom, also my son Dylan's mom, is Mauritian. Although light skinned, by blood, she is a black/island mix.

Kids don't care about these issues when they're young but as they grow up, the main issue for all the kids is "where do I fit in?" Twenty-five now, Lucille has had a lot to deal with from the start.

I was raised with all the hugs and juicy kisses from my grandfather and mother, so that's what I know and do. Besides, it feels good. Lucille was born into her parents' turmoil. They were having a rather standard dissolution of their marriage before, during and after she was born.

So, for a lot of reasons, Lucy was more guarded and less of a touchy/feely kid. I had to learn how to back off, not take offense at her keeping her distance (that took awhile) and still be a parent and as much of a father as she would allow.

I had to learn that that was different than the fathering I wanted to offer. She saw things differently. She was having her own life experience.

My mom used to say that each child is an "only" child. I know that what she meant in her street PhD way, was that each child, each person, is unique. We, as parents, need to help our kids embrace their own uniqueness without being afraid of the differences they see in themselves.

There is no "one right way" to raise children. There are basics that apply across the board to safe childcare. But at the top of the list of learning how to be a parent (what school teaches that?), is the notion that your child will show you who he/she is and how they need to be guided. Thank you for the primer on that, Lucille.

Lucy's had her ups and downs and challenges like we all do; she's also had a harder road than some. She had a seizure when she was very young, she had a break down in her teens. There've been some very difficult, even frightening moments; anger turning the corner and getting out of control, going up to the borderline of safety. There's been a lot of work for her and the people in her life to do, to make progress.

I didn't have the "jurisdiction" I would have liked with her, when she was younger. Her mom didn't back me up, back then, when it came to discipline and boundaries. We differed in our expectations and demands. These are the issues we all run into as we combine partners and kids and pets. Married or not.

And at times, Lucille has made it hard to help her when she gets defensive over changing a habit that would improve her life, or thinking about some issues differently that would help her grow. Does any of this sound familiar?

But there's been no giving up (when you're a parent, you're a parent for life, is the way Tim Craig of Children's Circle School put it), we keep coming at the idea of "how do we get along in life" from different angles.

And now, she's working on the issues, day by day, making small but meaningful steps forward. And she's taught us both that as difficult as things can be, for whatever the reasons, when people care about what happens to each other in a meaningful way, and do some work and waking up, good can come of it.

Just recently, she booked an evening for us to go see *I Am Sam* together. She'd already seen it but wanted to see it with me as part of what we refer to as the "Week Long Birthday Celebrations" (she was turning 25). It's a very moving story of an autistic father who gets a homeless woman pregnant and is then left to raise the child on his own when the woman runs off as they leave the hospital.

At one point, the child welfare people put her with a "normal" foster couple. The child's love and devotion for the father, aside from what's natural, transcend the boundaries of intelligence. The little girl keeps finding her way back to the man who read her *Green Eggs and Ham,* hundreds of times, because that's all he could read. She had grown past him intellectually, but would be with him forever in her heart, because she knew that he cared about what happened to her and did what he could to be there for her.

Lucille is finding her way back to some of the sweetness she has always had in her heart that had gotten hidden away. I knew it was there all along and kept aiming for it, as we danced around the issues. She's believing it now too.

And she is still teaching me what it means to be a father.

Dance

Giant Leaf and Peace

A giant leaf
with a sun
dreaming about rain

and peace underneath
that can't be
taken away

Who's Teaching Who What?
An Introduction to Fatherhood

The teacher and the taught together create the teaching. —Eastern saying

It started out with fascination, which is where all the best knowing will come from. The mind goes to what charms it, we are told by Deepak Chopra, and the incredible reality of life forming itself in our midst, with or without our help, began my transformation, I think, into Fatherhood. The message it gave was, I am responsible but not in control.

I had read that the fetus can hear in the mother's womb and that the mother's heartbeat, actually sounding like a steel mill to the inhabitant when played on tape, can lull a nursery of crying infants to sleep. So, my "Daddying" began goofing with my wife's belly.

I'd do what a lot of first time fathers probably do: get close to the bulge and talk. I also sang a little. Then I took it to the next level and put really good headphones face down on the cave and played Stevie Wonder and Beethoven.

Later during the pregnancy, I'd find the feet with my fingers and we'd dance and push up against each other, my unborn son and I. "Let the wild rumpus begin," to quote a book by Maurice Sendak I would later read a zillion times.

I've always loved the work I've done making music. The business part is the most difficult, but the magic that can be created when the song moves you to move another person, is what it feels like to be connected to the universe and all that's in it. Music, my teacher told me, is immediate transportation to the infinite.

When my kids were born, I was there, like a lot of fathers. It was the most overwhelming experience of this I've ever had. As my son was being born and I watched the doctor assist, I felt this was the only thing in the world I'd want to do other than affecting people with music. Life assistant.

Dylan's birth was an induced labor. A precautionary and blessed ultrasound at 8 months (Patricia—Dylan's Mom—had lost a child at birth in her first marriage), showed that the umbilical cord was crimped, so we were told they would induce labor immediately.

This was Patricia's third delivery, but I was the novice, in every possible way. I'd diligently paid attention in the Lamaze classes, packed my bag and had it ready by the door to move at a moment's notice. The guerilla warrior, poised to get an "A."

And here we were, already at the hospital,

checked in with no supplies. I started hyperventilating, my thoughts flooded together. Of course I was panicking somewhat—what if there are complications? Maybe this is *serious*. The tenuous, fragile nature of life sprang up in my face, taunting me with its delicacy.

I didn't know what to *do*.

After a few moments of free fall, I approached the doctor who was monitoring the baby's heartbeat. With the slightly glazed, bug-eyed stare of confusion and mild hysteria, I said the only thing that came to mind, "We don't have our overnight bag." The doctor, the veteran, the combat seasoned professional turned to me calmly and said, "Well, go get it."

I ran from the hospital, got in my car and drove in what seemed to be an under water slow motion movie. The half hour ride took forever. I went to an ATM and took out my last $50. And despite all the turmoil, uncertainty and madness of living swirling around me, I knew that this was one of the happiest days of my life.

When I dashed back into the hospital room with pillow, overnight bag and cassette machine, deathly afraid I'd miss the birth of my first child, there was the doctor. Easily, calmly he was watching the baby heart monitor. My wife was at rest in the bed. I hadn't realized he would wait for me to come back, before he started to induce. Labor would be a push button event.

That was a pivotal point, for me, in becoming a father. I realized, we men feel we have to *do* something, know something, make something happen, when in fact, it is the women who are doing and knowing and making everything. And they are doing it with god, not us.

It started to dawn on me, ever so slightly, that I was a shepherd, a guide. I'm not steering anything, I'm not making anything happen. I'm a protector, an overseer. Sure, I can coach in the breathing and be a support. I was told I might get yelled at (that didn't happen until later). I could hold a hand and be encouraging. I could change the music.

And, in fact, those are the things we must do in all the days that follow. Oh there's the grunt work of wiping butts and walking the floor in the middle of the night, bouncing a helpless bundle so it might find comfort in this strange, airy, out of the water world.

But that is where we start to know that someone else is more important than we are. It doesn't matter if we're tired, someone else needs caring. Oh sure, we do it partly to stop the unnerving crying. But if we listen to our hearts, we'll hear it whisper to us, to go help someone else, too. Use the shoulders, carry someone else's weight.

As our main job, in our right minds, that's what fathers do.

Forget about likes and dislikes. They are of no consequence.
Just do what must be done. This may not be happiness, but it is greatness.

This is the true joy in life. The being used for a purpose, recognized by yourself as a mighty one. The being thoroughly worn out before you are thrown on the scrap heap. The being a force of nature instead of a feverish selfish little clod of ailments and grievances, complaining that the world will not devote itself to making you happy.

—George Bernard Shaw

The Angel of Mercy and the Harvest Moon

It flies and flies
in circles
because it likes
to play

and it
guards the
harvest of mercy

God Is My Dance Partner

teacher to kindergartner: *What are you drawing?*
kindergartner: *I'm drawing god.*

teacher: *But nobody knows what god looks like.*
kindergartner: *They will in a minute.*

Swaying and skipping, floating with the invisible infinite. That's pretty much my idea and experience of god. So, of course, that's what I talk about with my kids.

The "animating principle behind all things" is how we talk about the untalkable; it's how we talk about god. "The loving intelligence of being," is what Dr. Bernie Siegel calls it.

The Indians think of the natural world, the earth as sacred, Buddha talks of enlightenment, Jesus talks of love, Moses tells us of a way to act with each other, the Dalai Lama speaks of compassion, Lao-Tzu tells us of the way of all things.

These are many ways of saying what can't be said, of talking about what can't be talked about. I call it the "Tomato Seed Philosophy." Every time you try to put a finger on it, it spurts out across the plate. Religion is man-made, the spirit is what moves us—to dance, to tears, to laughter. The spirit is what is spurting across the plate. It's never "what you call it," Wayne Dyer explains.

Call it Buddha, Moses, Jesus, Mohammed, Lao-Tzu, the wind, the sun or the rain, the emphasis in our neighborhood is being grateful for this life we have with each other. What's important is to treat ourselves and each other kindly and with respect. How we act with each other is the issue. Be like you would want someone to be with you.

It's how we live and how we treat each other that matters most, in the end. I've heard other experts say, "How am I loved?" and "How did I love?" is what we'll think about at the end of our lives. Why not think about it here and teach our kids about it now?

Our approach to spirit, religion and the divine is: inclusion. My upbringing was Jewish. The Dalai Lama's message of compassion and about how we need to treat each other is the essence of all religions. The teachings from the east and the mystics describe the indescribable, about how we are miracles in the middle of the miraculous natural world and universe.

Somehow the kids seem closest to this "animating principle." Given half a chance, they're just delighted by life. Our idea is that like the fish that doesn't know it's in water, we don't know we're in god. A dolphin is doing just what it needs to do, swim with abandon and raise its young, snack on plankton or other local cuisine, stay away from hooks and nets. It would seem doing that, is its way of doing god's work.

And maybe that's what we need to do more of: swim with abandon (more jumping flips out of the water might do us all some good), attend to our young and eat more food from the sea.

But we can do something the dolphin may not be able to do; we can *know* we're swimming in god.

So our idea of doing god's work is natural and simple: be grateful for what we have, take care of ourselves and care about what happens to each other, be kind, have courage and talk about how we feel. It may not be organized but it is a way for us to go about our business living the universal ideas.

This is where it matters to us, how we are *moved* by the spirit of being human, what can we *do*, while we're here, to leave the place a little nicer than we found it.

We think this is what god has us here to do and, one way or another this is what we get to talking about, when we talk about god. We think this is what makes us happy, so this is what makes god happy. We agree—we're all in this together. How could we NOT be?

The current side effects of thinking that we're separate are a world torn apart by misery and delusion. Still, after all, these are the mysteries and, no matter what, they remain mysteries. This is where the magic lives, in the unknown. The caterpillar into a butterfly is best described as a natural wonder of god, as is a hummingbird or a dolphin. And while we can marvel, we can't explain the magic they hold for us. They are some of the more colorful and playful examples of the wonders of the mystery of life. And it is staying with this unknowing that keeps our lives a living ballet. There's no need (or way) to explain our connection with infinity (quantum physics and mystic insight can allude to it), there's most importantly, our need to *know* that we are connected to infinity and we need to live like we are.

Our human imagination is the wonder of god.

So, how do we live knowing we are connected to invisible infinity? Well, we start by thinking and talking about it. And, since we're talking about infinity, there are no boundaries. We don't edit the god talks we have. They're wide open. All ideas are welcome, nobody's right. Just different ways to talk about forever and a knowing that we all want the same things: to love and be loved. To have a good time.

We do it by being fully in the present moment and noticing the magic right in front of us. This, we think, is what the message from all these great people is, about how to do god's work. This is how we swim in god.

India's mom and Lucille's father are Christian. Dylan's mom was raised Catholic. I've got a laughing Buddha on the mantelpiece, we light the Chanukah candles and talk a little, about Jewish history, we talk about meditation and being kind and peaceful; we have a Christmas tree. It's nice to have a tree with lights in the living room.

India pretends she's the Buddha and when she sits in a meditation pose, asks, "Who's more calm, Daddy, me or the Buddha?" She gets in a little snit when I tell her it's a toss up.

She wears a cross necklace, sometimes, that her mom gave her and made a bead drawing of the yin and yang sign from the one I gave her. God, for Dylan, is probably closer to an NBA player, than anything else. It's good to study someone that has motion savvy and knows how to fly. He's a sensitive kid and knows a lot about love and caring.

The way we think and talk about it, god is everywhere, all the time. How could it be any other way? Do we really think god is going to intervene in our lives just because we whine or beg about it? We are the ones that are intervening in god's life, and if we're lucky, we'll know it, and have respect.

"Be deserving of the love you would like to receive," to quote my psychiatrist friend, Dr. Boyd. Again, these are not new ideas, what we bring to them for ourselves, is in what we *do* about these "ideas of god." We bring god to life by how we behave with each other. Of course, sometimes we forget, and we don't act well. But what we return to remembering, are these decent and kinder ways of being with each other.

This leaves plenty of room for unrestricted dialogue which, at times, can be very creative, funny and to the point. Kids on god can be hilarious, hugely insightful and enlightening. They can reconnect us to at least a glimpse of divine knowing—if we let them. There's no right or wrong for this at our house, it's just our way of finding god. Whether we know it or we don't, no matter what we call it, married or not.

Poetry is god's dialect.

We were hanging out and India decided she wanted to write a postcard to god and ask him for wings. I told her that sounded like a great idea. She asked me what goes where on the little make-'em-yourself postcards.

I said, "After where it says To: you put god."

And she asked me how to spell it.

I said, "The 1st letter is G,"

She writes G and says, "G, like dog?" to which I said, "Yes."

She says, "Then?" and I said, "O."

And she says as she writes, "O, Like dog?"

And the same thing happens with the D. And

then she says, "Hey, this is dog." And I said, "Well, it's the same letters, they're just in different places."

And she looks at it and says: "The difference between god and dog is the letters are in a different pointing."

She then goes on to make a delightful card, took the direction on how you visualize to create things and wrote a note that says:

Dear GodLoveYou

Thank you for my wings *(She's quite willing to accept the central idea that she must think and feel as if she's already got them, to get them. Easy for kids, hard for adults.)*

And later we're talking and I remind her that the place this all starts is in your mind. I tell her, "You need to close your eyes and get a very good and clear picture of what you look like with your wings and what your wings look like."

And she does this for a minute and then says, "I can't see anything," and then, "Oh, I see them," and then they must've slipped away, because she says impatiently (a holy valley princess),

"I don't care *what* my wings look like, I just want to fly."

I told her she was doing great spirit work and asked, "Do you know what spirit work is?" She said, "No."

I told her that's when you think about how god is like you and how you are like god.

She says, "Well, I think about god all the time," and I said, "I can tell, it shows on your face."

There is a story from a workshop run by the teacher and mystic, Stephen Levine.

A young couple had been consulting with their therapist regarding what they considered a rather odd request from their three-year-old daughter. As the mother neared the end of her pregnancy, her daughter repeatedly asked to speak to her newly arriving brother or sister, *alone*.

The little girl was very persistent in her heartfelt request and it lead her parents to believe that it must carry some true importance for her. She was a normal and gentle child, and since the couple had an intercom system in their home, they and their therapist agreed to allow her this request when the new baby seemed settled in their home. So, after several months of these repeated desires to speak to the baby alone, they allowed it.

When the baby boy was a few weeks old, the little girl asked her mother if she could have her special request. The mother agreed and the parents dashed into their bedroom to listen closely on the intercom.

They heard their daughter walk to the crib and in hushed, urgent and reverent tones, they hear the little girl say to her infant brother, "Baby, baby, *please* . . . tell me about god! I'm starting to forget."

As we move with the invisible infinite, why not let the kids lead sometimes, in a dance with god?

3 on a Bench

3 friends, who
know
and
they don't know
what they like

Just Say Know

Everybody is ignorant, only on different subjects.
—Will Rogers, actor and humorist (1879–1935)

The biggest problem we have with children, is ourselves. I've done it the biggest. Can't just be friends—got to be the boundary. And . . . got to be there to do that. So we're back to square one: presence.

I just call help. The Grammas and Grampas are less and less around. Many uncles and aunts do what they can, when they can. My own mother used to say, "Knock on any door, you'll find everyone's got their troubles." I have a friend who's raising his son's kid. The family we've heard about or had, is just as susceptible to the same issues, that other families, blended, step, single-parent, extended, rehabilitated experience.

So, when pondering the influences and confluences from the people in our lives, it's good to consider that: "They did the best they could with what they had." We got some of it, some good, some bad.

I just figure there are those more objective, with insights and experience, that could offer some vision into what to do, *how* to know, what things mean, options that would be good for a kid and a parent. Sage advice. It works for me.

I'm talking about the elders and all the other input, wisdom, counseling, whatever you want to call it. Another opinion. Getting some perspective, getting a grip. Getting a ref.

Save some time; ask someone who knows. "You gotta go there, to know there," Nora Zeale Hurston describes it so eloquently.

This all requires a certain humility in accepting that we *don't* know everything and we're *NOT* always right.

And who better to test that in us, than our children? We were never taught these things anywhere else. We know that the people we invite into our lives, are our teachers. The angel babies are some of the most profound ones.

So the wisdom we can bring, comes from the neighborhood, the village (more and more, an extended family) that it *does* take, as the African proverb sings, to raise a child. We need to know things we had nowhere to learn but here. And the knowing we can find, we are here to learn from each other, as the Kabbalah says, "how to love better and to grow in wisdom."

My experience is that the kids are god's way of bringing you more into life, if we let them, if we let ourselves.

We all need a good teacher. Find one and start learning.

We don't know everything, and we're not always right.

We have much to know, and we learn from our mistakes.

There we go. That was easy. Start there.

A Buddha

A Buddha
that is
meditating

and
floating in the air
to see
what it's like.

It says

"I don't know what
abandoned means."

2-Wheel Metaphysics

Let our opportunities overshadow our grievances.
—Booker T. Washington, educator and writer (1856–1915)

Learning how to balance on two wheels was a delicate rite of passage in the spring.

There we were, faced with the ancient tradition of subtly mixing balance and coordination, unaided, in the wind.

The only way to do such complex adventures is by not thinking about how you do it. The learning, in this case, comes from body know-how.

But we usually interfere with this innate knowing by telling ourselves some kind of negative story about why we can't do whatever it is. And, over time and a lot of repetitions, we believe it. Seems to be a natural human inclination.

So here's India, wanting to ride her two-wheeler without training wheels, so bad, she can taste it. Chomping at the pedals.

And, of course, I know she's ripe for one of life's grand rituals, a personal experience in the fancy-free use of the wheel.

True to script, we were set: the training wheels removed, we went off down the street to do this. Or, at least, to start it. I heard the heroics of John Williams music, swelling in the background.

India is fit to be tied. She can't stay up without me holding her for a second. She's throwing a valley tantrum, whining, "I can't *do* this! I'll *never* get it. This bike is *stupid*. I'll *never* learn how to ride a bike."

Classic negative self-defeating drunken monkey commentary.

Of course, I couldn't pass up the opportunity for a teaching. So, Superdad that I am, I answered back to her, as she ran through her menu of self-criticism, "Well, you know, there's no need to say bad things to yourself about it. You'll learn much better and faster if you say things like: 'I can do it, next one will be better, I'm just going to keep at this, I'm getting it,'" you know, steady as she goes stuff.

I even told her the story of how when I was learning to ride a two-wheeler, I got so upset that I threw the bike down.

She was so upset that she didn't care and wasn't even paying attention. Usually kids love stories about how their parents really sucked at something. Not a peep, just a pout.

So I said we had to take a break, I was kind of spent from running down the street holding her up.

Of course, being still at this crucial moment was nearly impossible and it was from that impatience that India started pushing herself along, slightly, with her feet.

Sensing the wind picking up there in the ocean, I caught her, for just a nanosecond, gliding from one of her little self-inflicted shoves and shouted, "That's it!"

Then she stopped and started her goose walk, and straddling her bike, went into another, slightly longer glide and catching her at it again I called out, "You're doing it!"

At this point, we arrived at the video store, the original destination. I went in for a tape and India stayed at the front door, the fantastic events of the last few minutes swirling through her body and mind. She was processing like crazy, I could hear her thinking it over from across the store.

As we left the store, India shoved off and glided right down the sidewalk and around the corner. When I caught up with her, she had stopped by an alley—the moment was upon us.

I looked around. There were no cars. So, I told her to go ahead.

She pushed with her feet; started to glide. And then her feet found the pedals and my six-year-old little girl swept herself into an infinitely expanded universe, forever.

As she moved down the street, tentatively but truly, holding her balance, or letting her balance hold her, I shouted out, *"Keep pedaling, keep gliding and keep having fun!"* Yet again, we'd stumbled upon one of life's great truths.

India rode with great exuberance flashing off her pink helmet for 1 block before she stopped, turned to me, as I rode up, her entire being aglow, and said, "Daddy, I *did* it."

Crossing the anonymous and momentous milestones in our lives so resoundingly, can give us the grounding and courage to face our continuing life dance with its more complex steps. None of us need to take our setbacks with us forever but our triumphs can carry us through our entire lives.

I wanted to take a moment to savor and reflect on this life passage with India. I wanted to make a small but real life-moment highlight of the event. She had created the perfect opportunity to finish the teaching.

So as India stopped in the street to enjoy her glorious achievement, I walked over to her and said, "Well, you learned two things today."

"First, you learned how to ride a two-wheeler without training wheels," I said intently.

"And second, you learned that there's no need to say bad things to yourself when you're learning something new."

"As a matter of fact," I added with great enthusiasm, "it went better when we said a few good things."

India paused, and gave me her "I'm well aware of this" look and said, "I *knew* you'd say that."

Staying with the pleasure of just being together in our life dance, and paying attention to the little steps, we found ourselves riding on a metaphysical bicycle built for two.

MAGNA

Cat

Two kitties
love each other
very much,
really.

They went to dinner,
kissed and
made a tree with
artwork
from
faraway places

CAT

Stay Together for the Sake of the Kids

Life has taught us that love does not consist in gazing at each other but in looking outward together in the same direction.
—Antoine De Saint-Exupery, writer (1900–1944)

The simple truth is, whatever we parents may have going on in own lives, separately or together, the best thing we can do for our kids, is for us as parents to find a way, in this vast and surprising universe, to actually like each other. Married, or not.

Now I know there are circumstances where you'd say there is no way that could ever happen. Truth is, these are the most common stories. We hear them every day. But is that the end of the story?

The point, I think, is that if we relax for a minute and take the responsibility for giving care and kindness (and what better place to start, than with a child) to the foundations of our society, using hearts and minds as big as we can make them, we see that everybody wins.

This is the starting point. Parents harbor such great creative potential to the forming of the world. We could have the groundwork for the brave new place we all seek, knowingly or by chance. What if we were suspicious enough to try really caring, because we want there to be a wonderful world out there, if only for the kids? Maybe our caring and attention could be a strong part of the world, something to count on. It could be contagious. Just as the inattention and carelessness is. And what if we find out that we've done it for ourselves? Any Universal information will tell you the same thing: caring for someone else, IS caring for yourself.

T-shirt: Like Someone You've Divorced or Alienated in Some Way

It starts in any family, with whatever parents are around. We find a way of getting over our differences enough, to care about what happens to a kid.

I hear people saying, "Yeah, right." Well, yeah, right. Do it. What if it works? What if it even works a little?

If we had even a little respect and decency, and at least *thought* about being good to each other and ourselves, we might discover our children, too, have changed. And one way we can do that is to give ourselves the gift, of finding a way to get along with someone we had a kid with but don't want to be married to anymore. Dropping the fear and anger makes it possible to create a chance that our kids won't have to carry it too.

Does it happen? Sure. Not as often as it could. Not as often as we need. Pass it on.

My kids have two different mothers. We've had shouting matches, angry exchanges, hung up the phone on each other, made threats of calls to lawyers, made calls to lawyers, the "full catastrophe," as Zorba would say. These scenes, and their underlying causes, are some of what lead to our parting ways. But the "full catastrophe" is what we carry with us also.

And through it all, to everyone's great benefit, we've stayed in communication (the only time good works can get done is when tempers are calm), and reoriented ourselves to the goal of finding a way to co-operate with each other, to "stay together for the sake of the kids." We have let this mutual regard for our children, lead the way to what can be described as a respect and regard for decent interaction, on behalf of the kids, and ourselves. I have always been inclined to do what can be done to work things through, somehow, so I would also say, that this interaction leads us towards a fondness for each other. Our kids get to carry that too.

Kid issues are immediately and the most of all, human issues. You can't give something you don't have, to someone who needs it more. If I don't have a nickel, I can't give you one, no matter how badly we both need one. Funny though, with love, caring and compassion; if you give it first, law of the universe, you'll get it given to you.

So the idea we do our best to keep in mind is that, our best gift to the children, ours, or anyone's, is if we can find a way to care for ourselves *and* each other, in spite of what's happened between us. *Because* of what's happened between us. Because of what *could* happen between us. The idea is so close at hand, I find myself, as I recognize the notion of this "mutual aid society," as a fish, screaming, "Water!" We're in it and we don't know it. Our children need us to know this, and respect *them* enough, to act like this with each other. This is the emotional foundation they need. It is the one we all need. That is what, if we're lucky, we'll find a way to do, for our kids. And we'll find out we've done it for ourselves.

T-shirt: Find a way to be, together.

So, here we are, at the seat of all religions: Do unto children of all ages, as you would have children of all ages do unto you.

Dancing Cat

She's a weirdo

She
    got her nose pierced
She got her
    ears pierced
but she's dancing
    anyway

Metaphysical Bike Talks

Not knowing when the dawn will come I open every door.
—*Emily Dickinson, poet (1830–1886)*

India, her world expanded—because her mind expanded, since she learned how to ride without training wheels a week ago—has only been off the bike to sleep. And I'm certain while sleeping, she was dreaming of riding.

So I've fixed up the new bike we bought for Dylan, 6 years ago, just as he stopped being interested in bike riding, to hit the trails with India. The central activity at our house at this point, is finding a reason to go *somewhere*, so we can ride the bikes *anywhere*.

New repeated phrase: "Don't you have *something* you need to get at the grocery store?"

And on the two block trip home from the video store, "Let's play," as she rides up one side of the sleepy sloped street, then the other, now means, "Let's ride."

Riding brings out the flow and makes for fluid thinking and allows the imagination to stream in our minds.

And so, India starts her observations.

"Daddy," she says, "let's ride somewhere."

"Okay."

"Where should we go?" then answering herself, "Let's go a way we've never gone."

"All right," I said, "we'll go to the end of the street and then go right."

"Instead of going left like we did last time?"

"Yes."

"That's a good idea. Everybody always wants to go somewhere they've been and they need to go someplace new."

"I'm with you," I said, as we rode off.

Last week, when she first got it, she rode everywhere fast. Now, one week later, she's clearly enjoying the slow cruise. Balance is assured and confident, so she can amble. And not get home so fast.

"Oh, I see," I mention, baiting, "now you like to cruise slow. Last week you were going everywhere fast, now you like the slow glide."

"Yeah," she says, nonchalantly. "It's because, if you go too fast then there's things that you don't see.

"You need to slow down so you can notice what you might miss."

Who, is dancing with whom?

Time Out

How can I miss you if you won't go away?

What about discipline? And who needs discipline? What about solitude? And who needs to be alone? We, as parents especially, need these first.

Where do we learn about discipline and solitude? Our parents? Probably only sort of or somehow screwed up. That's OK—first impressions are what we're all working with.

Did we get appropriate guidance on how to control ourselves from Priests, Rabbis, Nuns, Teachers, Relatives, Friends? Are the movies and TV where most of the input comes from? Are there a generation of guys out there who have learned how to implode like James Dean?

Who told us about the value of being still? How did we learn to calm ourselves down? Have we learned to calm ourselves down?

Taking the inventory, do we find gaps in our education and knowing? As the observers we must be, do we see areas that might be lacking in effectiveness and usefulness?

How does it get beautiful around here, if we don't make it beautiful ourselves?

Any dance requires "the discipline it takes" to repeat the same moves, over and over, until they're done with ease and then can be communicated by their beauty of motion, undistracted by thinking. That's just how we learn and "know" something. It becomes, "second nature."

The same goes for our raising children or ourselves. Only what we need to consider, is that we need to guide ourselves, over and over, so we can guide the kids, over and over.

Kids learn what they live and everybody's in the test tube. Married or not. So we all influence the results, by whatever we do, or, *don't* do.

So it's up to us to *be* the control, we'd like to see our kids have. And how do we do that?

On-going education is basic. There is a list of books, movies, groups and web links under "Resources" at the end of this book.

On the other hand, knowing and acting on the importance of *not* doing is also central. Having time when everybody is separate from each other, is one way that's rarely attended to.

Who among us, takes the time to sit quietly, alone, on a regular basis? If we want to help other people, we need to start with ourselves. The more rested, focused and healthier we are, the more we laugh. The more we're able to concentrate and articulate our visions and truths—and act on them—the more good we can do for ourselves and each other.

Teaching, by living the value and practice of

Santa Claus Is Jewish

he's at the
bar mitzvah

he's thinking
about

if he should leave

or stay

because he got up
on
the wrong side
of
the bed

everybody needs to rest
sometimes

solitude and peacefulness as part of our daily lives, is a valuable guideline in our house. Does it happen all the time? Not a chance. But it's a pointing, an orientation, they're some of the things that happen around our house.

It's a matter of scheduling. But this is scheduling "alone time." And, as Pascal has remarked so concisely, "Most of humankind's troubles, are due to his inability to sit quietly in a room by himself."

This all starts with our *own* knowing.

One thing we need to know more about, is the power of our own council and reflection. Solitude gives us the chance to let the activity come to rest, to let it sort and settle. This is just as dreams are the soul's way of making sense of the nonsense (or more like, nonsense out of the senses), during our paralyzed still sleep.

We need to be still (or learn how) so our children can learn to be still: More meditation and personal time, less sugar and TV. Maybe this would lead to less ADD. There are doctors that think so.

A muscle in constant use, will tire, then lose its usefulness and then become dysfunctional.

So, finding the ways to be calm in the face of the madnesses of life, is one of our central occupations. Peace in the midst of chaos is what health is. Yes, our kids will be out of control and we will need to help them regain it.

The best technique I've seen came from a psychiatric hospital, used for our purposes, with younger children from 3 to 8 years old.

We tell them while all's well, that if there's tantrum, out of control behavior, we'll have quiet time and they'll sit on our lap, just in front of a blank wall, for as many minutes as they are years old. And that if they move or talk during the quiet time, we'll add a minute. We use a timer that they can see and hear. We hold them lovingly, firmly but calmly at these times, until they're calm and returned to being at ease.

There's no humiliation, no shame, no shouting, no violence. We teach our kids that we are with them, holding them, especially in this moment when they feel so out of control. It can remove the hysteria and fear surrounding these intense feelings.

I've had to do this only twice with Dylan and once with India. The message of control in the presence of emotional wildness was a clear one. They got it easily and then it became the *words* about calming down that took on the power.

The idea of being held and calmed, had become physically what they were now able to do, in part, for themselves. At least we've established a way to relate to each other about the calming down. We still have dramas, just less dramatics.

Maybe we need to hold ourselves when the madness strikes. Take a moment, in a calm environment, alone and let the storm settle. Or just observe it instead of being consumed by it.

We need to find this for ourselves. It is then that we can and must give it to our kids and our world.

Beautiful Angel

Beautiful angel
with
the open arms
of love

Not Seeing Is Believing

The heart has its reasons which reason knows nothing of.
—Blaise Pascal, physicist and philosopher (1623–1662)

trusting in the
miniature moves
nature & the universe engender
as they conspire
to make
something
of us all,
is an imperceptible
to the
naked eye
progress
only made visible
by small things

We cruise the neighborhood, have our local stops, like everyone does. We treat a trip with a twinge of event status. One never knows what we'll find, even if we started out simply for a loaf of bread.

The different lives people carry around with them—sorrows, prides, defenses, loves ("we all get the faces we deserve") are always on full display and in concentrated form at the grocery store.

I used to carry Dylan in a pouch (it was tailored, at the time, so he could face forward) around the neighborhood at 4 A.M. We'd stop by the "Tree of Birds," a round heavily leafed tree with what sounded like hundreds of birds chirping, mutedly in the pre dawn.

We'd then go on and end up schmoozing with the guys in produce at Ralph's.

We've lived in the same house since Lucille was six, and where Dylan and India were born. That is less a usual occurrence these days. So a walk down the street is an ingrained adventure and has always had "promise of discovery" as part of the possibility tone to the very idea.

Our neighborhood routine walk (it can happen anywhere) makes us feel grounded and reminds us of the good parts of being together. And it offers us a fine opportunity to do just that, be together.

It was on one of these walks that India revealed some of her clear understanding of connectedness.

One of my favorite prayers goes, "From your mouth to god's ears." My mom used to say that when I'd describe my fantastic plans. This happened my whole life. In the end, I can see, I took it as an endorsement. I've always had fantastic plans. Some have worked out, some haven't, but we've had fun and done some good.

One of my fantastic plans, is that my kids will have the memory and whatever knowledge possible, of their beloved elders. They'll be able to choose who those are, as they grow up; which wisened ideas appeal to them.

I have chosen to remind them of their grandmother. Lucille, India and her cousin Lilly, my youngest brother Gary's daughter, another bright beauty, were Alice's girls. My fantastic plan is to help keep that love alive with all her grandchildren and especially in the three girls' hearts.

So we talk about silly-good things we did with Gramma (teaching her to meditate, funny photo poses at the pizza parlor), what she liked (the hugs, kisses and emotional brilliances), what she used to say on the phone when there wasn't anything else to say and she just wanted to linger, "Yeah . . . and . . . so. . . ."

We also talk about how much she loved us all.

One of the trees that India and I have appreciated on the way to the store is a Jacaranda. The deep brilliant green delicate fossil-like leaves and dreamy lavender blossoms make it an easy choice. Their subtle beauty waves effortlessly and stands out in an overture to spring's delight, all over town. We, at that time, are often on Jacaranda patrol.

On this particular stroll, it was winter, there were no blossoms as we passed our tree.

Struck with a thought, I pointed out to India that the purple flowers we love were still part of the Jacaranda tree, even though we couldn't see them. She said, "I know."

With this easy connection, I then said, "It's just like Gramma. Even though you can't see her . . ." I paused and India filled in, ". . . she's still there."

A very wise and wonderful friend of mine, Dr. Boyd, the most realized man I know, who masquerades as a psychiatrist, once said, ". . . and after all, where do people exist? In large measure, they live in our hearts."

India shows us what belief is, as she knows that love is alive in her heart.

On the way home, as we passed our Jacaranda, it was as if Alice had come out to validate our thoughts of her, we saw one lone violet blossom on the top of the tree, swaying gently in an early evening breeze.

It seemed to say, "Remember and believe this love."

Game Heart

This is
a Heart that
loves a game

no eyes no nose no mouth

this is a Heart
that talks
and loves
the games

Be Careful, There's a Baby in the House

Sticks and stones can break my bones,
but words can break my heart.
—Robert Fulghum, clergyman and writer

97% of all communication is non-verbal. We've heard this before. This leaves us with little ET's around the house that, indiscriminately, soak up all that goes on. They just can't explain things away, the way adults do.

That automatically leaves *us* mandated to be observant and watch to see how we are behaving. Or not. These are some of the greatest lessons our kids can give us: a true glimpse of ourselves at the subtlest of levels.

From the slightest whim of emotion, to body language, to thinking, to how you close the refrigerator door, these little creatures emulate their caregivers.

So it can go either way. We can visit the mistakes from our past on them, by remaining unaware of habits we've picked up from who knows where, that keep us negative, anxious, fearful and stuck or, we can do something else.

It's just as possible to offer possibilities, as it is to criticize. Just as possible to encourage, as it is to be impatient and flare up.

It takes some work. We need to pay attention. So what. Why *wouldn't* we do it?

Make a play date. Do the stroll.

Which is what we did with Uncle Neil.

My brother is a wonderful man, who loves his nieces and nephews. He and his wife Lisa have no children of their own, their businesses are their kids. They have the kids over to swim in their pool and be the relatives—Uncle Neil is the quintessential shark.

And as gentle and caring as he can be, there was a time when his own joking and baiting, unwittingly bruised India in a way that highlighted, for me, the subtleties of the kids' (all of our) sensitivities.

And the way India ended up dancing with the issue, tossing it from many angles in her imagination, stands as one of the great anonymous-mini moments in mind play.

We all learned something. We all did the twist.

Uncle Neil, on a rare night on his own, came over to go out to dinner with me and India. She was three years old.

We were getting ourselves organized to go and India drew her name in the large capitol letters she uses.

Uncle Neil pointed to the word and asked India, "What does that say?"

She says, "India."

"OOhhhh!!" says Neil, "that's good." And then, pointing to the letter "I" he asks, "And what is this?"

To which India answers, "India." We weren't doing letters yet, she didn't know, her name was copied artwork.

And Uncle Neil, doing his best sarcastic clowning, said, "Oh. I thought India was a big girl. But I see she's still a little girl."

The psycho-drama of heartache instantly filled the room like an air bag in an auto wreck.

India, who has a great fondness for her Uncle —we know by now, she's a dearheart in general— was crushed.

After a few moments of head down silence (she is certainly processing as fast as she can go here), she says with a slight whimper, "Daddy. Uncle Neil said I'm a little girl, but I'm a big girl."

I knew I would fail at changing anything. I knew I would be labeled the overprotective father. There could be no damage control. So I thought, "Well, this won't work but here goes." And I said to India, "Well, sweetheart, Uncle Neil was just joking. You know what a joke is, don't you? What's a joke?"

"A joke is when somebody says something and you laugh," she says quite correctly. Clearly not laughing.

"Right," I said, "and Uncle Neil was just joking."

"I'm not a little girl, I'm a big girl," she said.

During the course of that evening, she came at the problem from many angles, even stumbling on the truth as she confessed, "Well, I *am* a little girl but I'm a big girl too."

India tugged at this life dilemma when we got together, not as intensely, over the next month. She had been given a Zen koan by her uncle and her mind was engaged.

About this time, on a shopping trip with Lucille, Dylan, and myself, India asked if she could have a cookie. I said sure, we'll just take care of Lucille's business first, then we'll get you a cookie.

While waiting to pay for Lucille's purchases, India asked, "Can I have a cookie?" I looked around and saw only packages of cookies. So, thinking a *little* sugar is OK, I reached for some M&M peanuts to share between us.

I asked India if she'd like some M&Ms instead of a cookie? As a veteran of Sesame Street *and* these wars, I know to use the word *instead* as many times as possible.

She, of course, immediately said yes. *Any* sugar is good sugar when you're craving and you've been patient.

So, every time I gave her an M&M, I said, "OK. . . . Here's another M&M, *instead* of a cookie!"

We walked back to the car, got in and snapped seat belts shut. As soon as the last click snips the air, India says from her car seat, "Daddy. I want a *cookie*."

Prepared for this moment, I turned to her and with great sympathy said, "But sweetheart, we had M&Ms *instead* of a cookie."

I could see her mind whirring, as she looked over at me and calmly said, "I was just *joking*."

From then on, there was a part of her I thought of as "girlfriend." A word.

Because . . . she was a little girl but she was a *big* girl too.

The Kitty of Sight

The kitty of sight

Can see anything
that she

wants to see

Life's Trick Connections

All knowledge begins with wonder.
—Goethe (1749–1832)

Morning routine, on a weekend: snuggle in bed. India comes into my room, a little gleam in her eye that says, "I'm here to start the fun."

This is float time, time out of time, just to be in the room.

We ramble, talk, goof, sit silently, one moment leading to wherever.

Off the clock.

Thumb wrestle turns to chicken tickle, then a pause, that settles into dream talks. This spills into daydream.

Then, while gazing at pictures beside the bed—we all have pictures beside the bed—India says, "Gramma."

"We were so lucky to have her," I pick up.

"How old was I when she died?" she asks.

"You were five. We love Gramma even more now than before, don't we?" I say.

"No," she says with wisdom, "we love her just as much."

"We were lucky to have her here, at home with us, when she died," I add. "Most of the time people are in hospitals, with people they don't know when they die. She was home with us."

India asks, "Does anyone in the world live forever?"

I say, "People can live in your heart forever."

"I mean, can anyone *live* forever?" she asks wanting to pin it down.

After a pause, I admit, "No."

Then add, "After awhile, we finish here and we go back to being an angel."

"Do you remember the story," I ask, "where before you were born, you were an angel and then you decided to come from where the angels are to be a person and you chose your mom and dad?"

"Yes," she replies, matter of factly.

"Well," I continue, "you come from being an angel to being a person and then when you're finished, you go back to being an angel."

"But when a person makes a beautiful drawing, or writes a beautiful song or poem or story, or smiles and is kind, and other people see that drawing or hear that song or poem or story, or remember the kindness, that person's drawing or poem or kindness will live in the hearts of other people. Forever."

"That's the art of a person," she says without hesitation.

Wondering around
we found
some of life's trick connections

Smile Anyway

She's at

a fun fare

and she's

daydreaming

about

daydreaming

Waiting Room

Life is like an ever-shifting kaleidoscope—a slight change, and all patterns alter.
—Sharon Salzberg, cofounder of the Insight Meditation Society

India and I waited at the doctor's for 2 hours the other day. She's such a good kid, even with a low-grade fever, she played and only half heartedly complained a few times.

I can be so engaged in our time together, I go into a time warp sometimes when we hang out. She enables me, or I enable myself (we enable each other), to slip into the timelessness of being a father in the foreverness of things, and these "small mundane" activities become infused with infinity.

It's like even as I was sitting reading a book, I had a mindfulness, a knowing, an observation of myself sitting there reading a book, in the doctor's office with India playing, watching her flow on the play stuff with one kid, and not with another.

It was like a present tense "experience" of *care giving* at the level of the *on going*—parenting as a path to enlightenment. We're playing out this ballet with each other as countless other parents and children have, in the summer/fall/winter/spring life Olympics. And it's our turn on the ice with the entire world as a backdrop. Only we won't be judged—we've already got the gold by just being here. And we represent all countries and all people everywhere, forever.

As I look at her I think, "Watch. This is how it's done. This is how life unfolds. This ice dance is a 10."

India's Jingle Bells (12/01)

Dashing through the snow

On a one horse self and sleigh

All the fields we go

Laughing all the way

Balls and cocktails ring

Making spirit's bride

What fun it is to laugh

and play with spiritses tonight

A Boy

He is
my favorite
he is
my brother.
he's a good
tickle monster
he's funny
and
action

A Brother's a Brother, a Sister's a Sister

"We will live together as brothers or die together as fools."
—Martin Luther King, Jr., clergyman (1929–1968)

Dylan is India's big brother. He is a dear, sweet, honorable, bright kid. He is also 14 years old and like most kids his age, he's got mood swings. But underneath and through all the stuff of the age, he's a fantastic kid with great integrity.

We are all lucky to have him.

And India adores him. He's really her main man. When he's around, I'm just the chauffeur and the waiter. We don't bother with traditional descriptions of step, or half brother or sister. We acknowledge what we're doing, we're a brother, a sister, a mother or father. Where everyone came from and who they might have left behind is real but secondary.

We do our best to pay attention to what's in front of us instead of what's behind us or what's coming. We've all talked from the beginning about how we're family; that we care about each other, wherever we live or who's married, or not, to whom. The idea has grafted and is working.

The general idea around our blended neighborhood is to act like nothing's "wrong." A brother does what a brother does, as does a sister or any other family member, to the best of their ability. We talk about what that means—and it's not too complex.

We share community property, we are reminded of and enact the little courtesies of life. Thank yous here and there. Saying bless you when someone sneezes. No big pressure, just a reflection on gratitude for what we have, that makes our life decent and sane. That's a lot.

Dylan was 8 when India was born. He was at the hospital, that first night, holding his sister's hand. She was transfixed with him. Tammy—India's Mom—Grandma Beverly, myself and Dylan, were thrilled to welcome this new creature into the world. That was our pleasure and focus.

Tammy and I weren't married, the pregnancy wasn't planned, nobody was financially secure. But it was a roomful of people caught in the delight of life.

Having raised Dylan as I had, I knew the long nights and hard work there was to come. In fact,

Tammy and I would part. But the theme throughout, has been to know the responsibility we had created with each other.

Likewise, we arranged for the kids to be with each parent and, at times, with each other. There is health in real community and we all are benefiting from it.

At this point, as Dylan and India have grown up "together," it's been different houses and different schedules. They're not with each other all the time or even every week. But the underlying notion is the same, and we allow that to guide us: they are brother and sister. We arrange time to goof and hang out, even though a teenager and a 6-year-old have very different interests. But this continued practice, having each other be in each other's life, on purpose, is how we operate.

Maybe *because* we don't all live together all the time, we're more able to appreciate each other. Oh sure there're snits and pouts and airs and dramas but they're in passing along the way to having fun again. That's the underlying agreement.

Maybe the differences in all the houses, makes our time together something of a curiosity. Maybe we have a chance to miss each other. Whatever the case, they crave belonging to this unit, whatever it is, very dearly.

These days, India and Dylan see each other less, but he has a soft spot for her and she still adores him.

Recently, one rainy Sunday afternoon, India and I picked up her beloved brother. India was quite excited at the prospect of having him to herself for some kind of boogie. "When we get home, will you play with me?" she asked, with heartfelt sincerity.

Dylan did not speak—clearly weighing his options: he likes her, she's cute, they do have some silly fun, a few minutes at a time. And he knew I wanted him to pay some attention to his adoring sister.

However . . . he also wanted to get onto the computer for some Instant Messaging with his friends. Now, we make it a point of valuing peoples' words. If someone addresses you, there must be a response. And so, after about 20 seconds of silence, India again asked, "Dyls, when we get home will you play with me?"

The air was thick with indecision. Dylan's racing mind fighting to analyze all needs.

"Will you?" his sister asked yet again. Leaning on his integrity and our "family agreement" that every inquiry will get a response.

After a few more anxious moments, the answer came: "We'll see."

And . . . after a beat, India replies, "Well . . . that's better than a no."

I was delighted, for them, for their regard for one another. A brother's a brother, a sister's a sister.

Just do it.

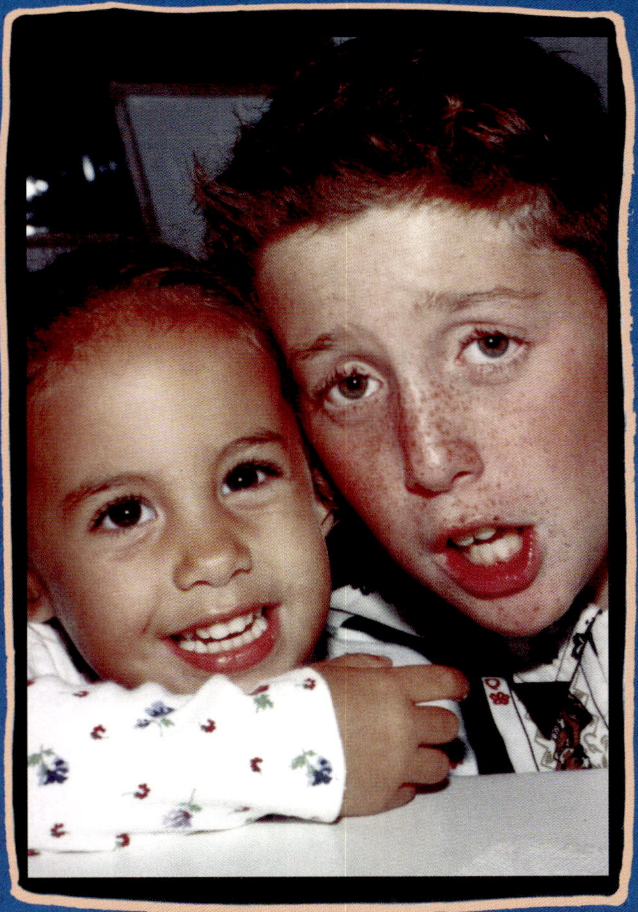

Glowing Tree

It's nighttime
and there's

a glowing tree
because
it has magical leaves
and

faeries live inside

because
they have to live
somewhere

Leaves

Heaven is under our feet as well as over our heads.
—Henry David Thoreau, writer (1817–1862)

India's spontaneity can be astonishing.

I think of it, sometimes,
jitter bug twist,
as spinning her out
'cross the floor
there's a gleam in her eye,
I think I know why,
when she lights,
she asks for more

enchanted, she goes,
neither one of us knows
what lies there
beyond the next dream
oh sure, yeah, I'll go there
heaven knows, I am told
there must be
something to see

So, I'm not a prison guard—there would be loud disagreement from my children, which is good, but we do trim down the TV and the sugar.

We're making "good" choices. We pay attention to eating good food, getting plenty of rest, taking vitamins, drinking the water.

And as a rule, "If you can't say nothin' nice, don't say nothin' at all," has worked well, as a guideline. Does it fail? Yes. But, we need guidelines. We have chocolate and ice cream, on occasion, because we love it like everybody does. There's nothing new here. We like to push the guidelines. But we have them.

The point is that, the more we actually *do* from the list of "Stuff We Know to Be Good for You," the better off we are. So, we aim to be flexible. Arbitrary, actually.

I learned that from Tim Craig, a wonderful Iron John of a man who owns and operates Children's Circle School in Van Nuys, the pre-school Dylan went to. His thinking is that the kids will come to learn, in a real way, that the parent is in charge, which is how they feel safe, which is basic to what we want most for them. When they feel safe, they can use their imaginations more of the time, instead of wondering if something is going to happen to them. Simple but true.

Tossing and jumping on the court, the pump ball dancers that we are, there are times, when we break routine; there's a small twist on an old idea. It can awe inspire in its immediate uniqueness: we do something different.

It can look like this: One day coming home from school, India asked, "Can I watch TV?" I hesitated for a second, thought about it, and answered, "Not now. Why don't you go play in the yard?" I'm exercising the aforementioned parental prerogative of being arbitrary.

Here it is: the sacred Moment. Does the kid simply do what the parent has outlined, do their own game, or whine and cry? These, pretty much, are the choices.

We all love it when everybody feels strong enough to make their own decisions.

India knew that the tone of voice meant "no TV now." Simple. She turned and went out into the backyard. A good time. We're on the same page.

There were leaves covering the yard, from large Chinese Elm trees, in November.

In the middle of fall. A basketball net, stationed in the middle of the asphalt ground.

India took a broom and swept the leaves into a pile to one side, making a play space for herself and leaving the basketball court clear. . . .

And then she got me
out of the house,
into the back, to see,
that the pile she had made,
no doubt of the shape,
was a heart
from her to me.

The Heart Knows Its Place

the heart
like a butterfly
can visit
wherever it wants

it
knows its place

The Love You Make

And in the end, the love you take is equal to the love you make.
—John Lennon & Paul McCartney

So, what do we learn, in the end, from our little earth walk?

What do we take from our time here with each other, with our children, our loved ones? What is important for the lives we live with the families we're born into, find ourselves in and the ones we choose?

We learn, if we're paying attention, that we're all in this together. There's no way to *NOT* be. That while it is good to receive, it is better to give. That giving *IS* receiving.

We learn that we all want the same things: to love and be loved, to feel safe. We seek pleasure and avoid pain. We want to know that someone cares about what happens to us. We want to be happy.

We want all this, in the end, so we can feel connected. We want to feel the connection with our children, our lovers, our parents, our friends, our co-workers, our country, our world and our god.

And the way we feel connected is by taking care of each other. When we take care of each other, it is how god takes care of us. Married or not.

There really are no rules for this to happen, there are only ideas that are good for children of all ages.

We all need, more than anything, to be appreciated for who we are and what we do. We need to sit quietly, at times, and not do anything about things. We need to appreciate ourselves.

We need to remember that we are partners here, no matter how you look at it and that by acting like partners is how we will find our own individual peace with ourselves.

We can fight about it and think that we know all there is to know and try and control our surroundings and other people, as we feel so out of control ourselves. And most of us do go, kicking and screaming, to enlightenment, to a new way of knowing. If we go at all.

Yet all of what we do here, in this ballet, is a way to dance out the love. Love for ourselves, our children and loved ones, our world. Everything is about love, as Don Miguel Ruiz says.

And finally, we're left where we began, with just being with each other mindfully, giving our attention and caring to each other, as the place to start.

Oh, we'll stumble and shout and forget and feel bad. We'll name call and eat too much sugar. We'll not put on sunscreen, stay up way too late. We'll get angry, we'll wish we were bigger.

But somehow, we'll remember.

We'll remember that life is a team sport. And the funniest thing, as Riane Eisler points out in her amazing book, *The Power of Partnership*, is that what matters the most, in any area of our lives, is the caring.

We need to wake up more to caring about ourselves and each other. This is where the magic comes from; this is where the changes will take place.

It will be, in the end, some kind person, from your own family, or someone else's, who will remind us to care for each other in a way that will finally make sense and click for us.

Here's one of those clicks.

India, Dylan and I were all in the living room one evening. No big deal, Dylan was on the couch making flash cards for a geometry test, I was on the computer and India was whirring next to the desk playing with one chachki or another.

Suddenly she took a pen and some paper and announced she wanted me to write something down.

She began by telling me to write: "I wrote a poem that kind of rhymes."

So I wrote it down. And then, quite delightfully, Dylan, the big 15-year-old—probably because he *wasn't* asked—came in with, "it turns back the hands of time."

They added a line here and there, we passed it around for "approval," agreeing, disagreeing and laughing.

What came of it is a simple treat, the results of nothing more than hanging out and being available to a couple of kids who had it in mind to be a little silly—but ended up being a little insightful and momentarily profound.

I wrote a poem
that kind of rhymes
it turns back
the hands of time
a story
about a little girl
who liked to twirl and twirl
and twirl
in her very own
funny world.

there's funny things
and funny places
where even babies have
brief cases
and funny clothes
that glow in the dark
making you a little smart
and heaven knows
you can find your way home
watching someone's dancing toes.

We get to where we're going by helping each other get there with the story that each of us makes for ourselves.

Make it a boogie woogie, and you can dance to it.

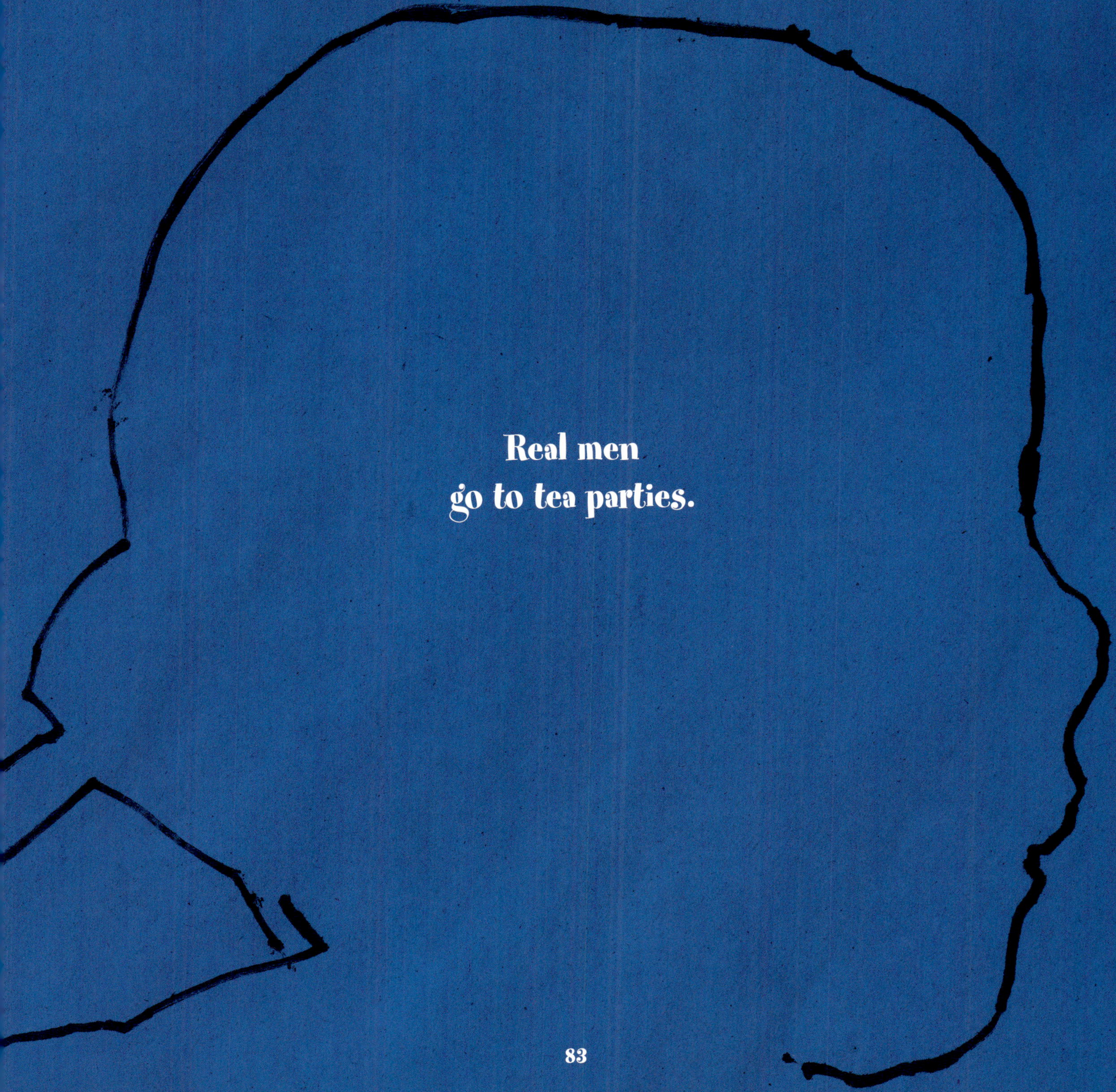

Real men
go to tea parties.

Resources

Movies

I Am Sam
Hearts in Atlantis
Life as a House
About a Boy
Two House Family
The Joy Luck Club
Erin Brockovich
You Can Count on Me
The House of the Spirit
Mask
Dead Poets Society
A River Runs Through It
Ordinary People
Tumbleweeds
Finding Forrester
Anywhere but Here
Hope Floats
To Kill a Mockingbird
Raisin in the Sun
Soul Food
The Heart Is a Lonely Hunter
Father of the Bride (Spencer Tracy/Elizabeth Taylor)
Angie
Grand Avenue
Smoke Signals
Medicine River

Books

Child & Family

Your Baby and Child by Penelope Leach

The Baby Book: Everything You Need to Know about Your Baby from Birth to Age Two by Martha and William Sears

The Happiest Baby on the Block: The New Way to Calm Crying and Help Your Baby Sleep Longer by Dr. Harvey Karp

What Do You Really Really Want For Your Children? by Wayne Dyer

The 7 Habits of Highly Effective Families by Stephen Covey

Parent Effectiveness Training by Thomas Gordon

10 Principles for Spiritual Parenting by Mimi Doe and Marsha Walch, PhD

Tomorrow's Children: A Blueprint for Partnership Education for the 21st Century by Riane Eisler

Stepwives: 10 Steps to Help Ex-wives and Stepmothers End the Struggle and Put the Kids First by Louise Oxhorn & Lynn Oxhorn-Ringwood

The Case Against Spanking: How to Stop Hitting and Start Raising Healthy Kids by Irwin Hyman

Reviving Ophelia: Saving the Selves of Adolescent Girls by Mary Pipher

Guide My Feet: Prayers and Meditations on Loving and Working for Children by Marian Wright Edelman

Personal Growth

The Heartmath Solution by Doc Childre and Howard Martin with Donna Beech

The Power of Partnership by Riane Eisler

The Four Agreements by Don Miguel Ruiz

You Can Heal Your Life by Louise Hay

A Return to Love by Marianne Williamson

Web

Blended Family Communities and Support

iStepfamily Magazine Online—The Original Magazine for Blended Families!
www.istepfamily.com

iStepfamilyJr!—The Original Online Community for Junior Blended Family Members—Ages 6–17!
www.istepfamilyjr.com

Our Blended Family—Interracial blended family information and support
http://go.to/interracialblend

Fathering Communities and Support

FatherMag.com—The Online Magazine for Men with Families
www.fathermag.com

National Center for Fathering—Conducts research on fathers and fathering and develops practical resources for dads
www.fathers.com

Center for Successful Fathering—Aims to increase awareness about the essential role fathers play in raising their children
www.fathering.org

Father's World—Information, resources, support, and education for fathers and their families
www.fathersworld.com

Stepparenting Communities and Support

The Second Wives Café—Online support community for second wives and stepmothers
www.secondwivescafe.com

The Stepparenting Connection—Non-profit corporation dedicated to assisting stepfamily; members find new friends, resources and support on the Internet and within their community
www.tsconnection.org

All Things Stepparenting—Newsletter and resources for stepparents
www.karongoodman.com/steps.html

StepDads.com—Resources and support for stepfathers
www.stepdads.com

Spiritual Healing for Blended Families

WholeFamily.com—Jewish family support site, including blended family issues
www.wholefamily.com

BlendingAFamily.com—Christian perspective on blended family life
www.blendingafamily.com

BlendedFamilyMinistry.com—Healing and hope for blended families from a biblical perspective
www.blendedfamilyministry.com

BeliefNet.com—Marital and family issues covered from an all-faiths perspective
www.beliefnet.com

Dance Card

The following pages are for taking stock of what goes on in your family-life and learning what "moves" you'd like to change, add or work on to make your own family-life boogie more fun or interesting or just different. Or not.

This is not a test and no one *has* to participate. Family, life, at it's best, is all volunteer work. Just keep in mind that there are no right or wrong answers, there are only better questions.

Good luck and remember, in the great words of the immortal Duke Ellington, "It don't mean a thing if it ain't got that swing."

If you'd like to contact Bill or India they can be reached at bill@angelmind.net.

Family Tree

Who are the members of your blood family (go as far back as you can go)? Tell stories anyone knows about them, see if you can bring them to family-life. What might it be like if they were here now? Who is in your blended or stepfamily (go as far back as anyone can go)? Tell stories about them (these don't have to all be nice stories). Can you imagine what family-life would be like if they were around? Who is part of your extended family and why? Who would you *like* to be part of your family? What makes you want them there?

What to Do?

What family activities do you generally have? Do you enjoy them? Who decides what they'll be? Can everyone contribute ideas on what activities there are? What different ones can you think of? How important is reading books in your family? What could you do without spending any money? How much of the time is the TV on in your house? WHAT WOULD YOU DO IF THE TV AND THE COMPUTER WERE TURNED OFF IN YOUR HOUSE FOR AN EXTENDED PERIOD OF TIME? How often do members of your family sit quietly and do nothing? What do you think would happen if you were still and quiet and did nothing for 20 minutes?

What Works

What do you like best about being in your family? What would you like to change? What do you like least about your family? What do you see in other families that you would like in your family? What can be done to change things? Are members of your family willing to change? Are they willing to learn how to change? What is the most fun you have in your family? How could there be more fun? How is the communication between people in your family? How could it be improved? What would an ideal family be like for you?

Make a drawing of your family.
You can use symbols and poetry.

Make a drawing of your dream of your family.
You can use symbols and poetry.

About the Artfuls

The odyssey of Bill Quateman continues to be unique and captivating. A native of Chicago, from the age of 14 he played a variety of music around town until, in the '70s, he began singing and playing in Windy City clubs and coffeehouses.

Shortly thereafter, Quateman was signed to Columbia Records, by legendary music impresario Clive Davis. There, he began building a devoted fan base following the release of his debut album, *Bill Quateman*, which led to critical acclaim, national tours and three albums for RCA.

A devoted single father of three, Bill has been raising his family in the Los Angeles area. A prolific writer, Quateman has created several multimedia projects, touching on some important and basic human issues.

His first book, a collaboration with his 6-year-old daughter, India, is a single father's blueprint and positive picture of a blended family that's having a good time and really works.

Bill is currently recording a new CD for release on his own web-based label. His self-titled album, *Bill Quateman*, and the previously unreleased *The Almost Eve of Everything* are now available on CD via his online music company, billquateman.com. He also maintains a humanitarian benefit effort, 4All of Us, that contributes a portion of profits to the EduCare Foundation (educarefoundation.com), an organization that educates kids, teens and adults in learning how to open their hearts and live more caringly.

India Rain Quateman, began drawing and singing, at the age of 2½. Her talents have been blossoming and she made her stage debut in Chicago in May 2002, singing with her father.

India lives half the time with her dad and brother and the other time with her mom, stepdad, step-brother, step-sister and new baby sister. Now 7, she is a 1st grader at Highland Hall Waldorf School. India continues to draw and sing, cartwheel and dance with serious whimsy and great abandon.

Bill and India can be reached at bill@angelmind.net.